MW01110045

Legacy Edition

IF GOD HEALS ...

Why Are So Many Christians Sick?

B. J. Willhite

Hisway Prayer Publications
P. O. Box 762
Jamul, CA 91935

If God Heals ... Why Are So Many Christians Sick?
Legacy Edition

ISBN: 978-1-879545-20-5

Publishers Note:

We all need heroes of the faith. We are very fortunate to have met Pastor Bob Willhite early in our ministry many years ago. Pastor Willhite became both our mentor in prayer and hero of faith. This great man's teachings on the subject of prayer radically impacted our lives and thousands of others throughout the U.S. and Internationally. "If God Heals" was written during a remarkable time in history when God was calling His people to prayer. (Ronald Reagan was President; the Berlin Wall was a focus point; and the Cold War was soon to end with the collapse of U.S.S.R.) National Call to Prayer began in Rockwall, Texas 30 + years and is still functioning to this day encouraging people to pray.

Our Reprinting this awesome book is to leave a Legacy of Prayer of this great man's teachings. You probably have never heard these principles of prayer anywhere else. They will encourage you, build your faith, and answer many of the questions you have had about prayer for a long time. You can listen to Pastor Bob's teaching at Hisway School of Prayer on most of the popular podcast platforms. Our prayer is that you will answer the call to prayer as we and thousands of others have.

One of the first principles that we learned from Pastor Bob was: "If you have enough faith to pray...you have enough faith to move the hand of God".

God Bless You,
John & Kathy Casto
Hisway Prayer Publications

About the author

B. J. Willhite was born in northwest Arkansas in the days of the old tri-state Pentecostal camp meetings and grew up under the preaching of men of God like Donald Gee and Raymond T. Richey. As a boy he saw platforms littered with crutches, braces, and wheelchairs and heard the joyful testimonies of the people who no longer needed them. Both of his parents were faithful praying people. His mother literally died on her knees while in prayer, and his aunt died in the same manner.

At the age of nineteen, B. J. Willhite fully committed his life to the Lord and to prayer. Hungry to know God, he often prayed from the conclusion of the Sunday morning service until time for the Sunday evening service to begin. Military service did not weaken his prayer life. His habit of beginning every day with prayer continued. In 1947 he married, and began preaching in 1949. Pastor Willhite recalls, "I knew that preachers, of all people, should pray: therefore, I set myself to develop more discipline in prayer than ever before." And pray he did, all through the twenty-eight years he pastored churches in Oklahoma, Missouri, Arkansas, and Texas.

In January of 1979, Pastor Willhite had just arisen from his knees and sat down at his desk when he heard the beginning of a radio broadcast – without the aid of a radio. He listened in amazement as a booming bass voice sang the theme song, "God of Our Fathers." Next, the opening announcements were made and the program began. At that moment the concept of a 300,000 member prayer army crystallized in his mind – an army that must be enlisted, instructed, inspired, and encouraged to pray through a national call to prayer. That vision became the driving force in his life.

Dedication

To Velma, my wife and prayer partner

For over seventy years

Contents

Introduction

This booklet does not profess to answer all of the questions which might be asked about why people are not always healed. In fact, it many raise more questions than it settles. However, my conviction for many years has been that God's people deserve more than a verse of Scripture out of context, or a pat answer to questions which produce doubt, inhibit their faith and trouble their minds.

It is my intent to help the reader gain a better understanding of God's eternal purpose regarding man. My prayer is that as y you read this message, God will grant you wisdom and spiritual comprehension, and that real faith based on a clearer understanding of God's will and His ways will be yours.

May those who suffer from illnesses which have not yielded to persistent prayer be encouraged to hold fast their confession of faith, while they submit to what may be God's perfect plan for their lives. I pray that we will all be able to say with the Apostle Paul: "I reckon that the sufferings of this present life are not worthy to be compared with the glory which awaits to be revealed in us." Amen!

B.J. Willhite

CHAPTER ONE

God's Design

If God heals, why are so many Christians sick and infirmed? Those who suffer from chronic or terminal illness and those who attend and pray for them have asked this question over and over. Is there an answer to this question? If there is, why has not more been written about it?

For some time it has been considered negative or unscriptural even to ask questions about problems which do to yield to 'pat' answers. However, the problems and questions persist and need a logical and scriptural answer.

To get to the root of the problem we must go back: "In the beginning God." This is the way God's revelation begins. A perfect God creates a perfect universe. At the close of every 'creative day' Scripture states that God looked upon what He had done and was pleased. Everything functioned exactly as it was designed. There was not evil in this creation; all was perfect. On the sixth day, God said: "let Us make man, and let Us give them dominion over all things in the earth. And God created man, male and female created He them and gave them dominion."

To this man, created perfect in every way, God gave the name of Adam. Eve, his wife was Just as perfect. She never needed to paint her face. Her complexion was perfect. Adam did not toil laboriously: the garden in which he and Eve were placed gave forth abundantly all they needed for their sustenance. There was peace in all of the earth: no pain, no sickness, no suffering, no death. It was paradise.

Adam and his wife lived in pristine innocence. They were no more inclined to do wrong than they were to do right. They possessed all things. Every animal was subject to them. There was only one prohibition: "the tree in the midst of the garden." Of that tree, God said: "You shall not eat. If you do, you will die...the very same day."

We do not know just how long Adam and Eve lived in the garden before they were tempted to disobey God's command. It could have been several years. One day Satan came to Eve in some subtle form and tempted her to eat of the fruit of the tree which had been forbidden them by God their Creator. Just how this temptation came about is not clear. Even what the serpent was like is not clear, but it was not then what it is now. Before the fall the serpent did not crawl on its belly. It may even have had wings. Who knows? All the Scripture says on the matter is: "The serpent was more cunning than any beast of the field which the Lord had made." That it could talk seemed normal to Eve. When the serpent begins to ask her questions she did not seem to be surprised. All seemed normal nothing out of the ordinary. Of course, from our vantage point we know some things Eve did not know.

We know Satan was in the serpent. Eve had no knowledge of Satan. As far as we know she had not been warned of such a being. Why? We can only speculate. Perhaps the knowledge of such a creature would have brought fear, shattering the peace and tranquility of the garden. All we know is what the Bible says on the matter. (There are times when brevity is dismaying to an inquiring mind.) I wish the Lord had given us more information about this matter. I am sure He would have if it would have been to our advantage.

Without going into a theological discussion of the various elements of the fall suffice it to say that when Eve sinned by disobeying the Lord and influenced her husband to do the same, everything changed. Suddenly, the whole world was different. Adam was affected in every area of his being: emotionally, physically, spiritually, materially, and morally.

Emotionally Adam **feared** – "We were afraid." Morally, he was feeling **guilt** – "We were naked...we hid ourselves." Spiritually, he was **separated from God** – "Where are you?" Materially, he was **put out of the garden** – "By the sweat of his barrow" he had to earn his living.

Physically, he **began to die**: from that very day, death begin to work in his body – "In the day you eat...you shall die." Paradise was surely lost. Health, wealth, fellowship, innocence – all were lost when Adam disobeyed God. What a price to pay for knowledge!

The moment Adam disobeyed; he knew evil and consequently knew good. One cannot really know good unless one knows evil. One can only appreciate light when one has experienced darkness. Sweet can be appreciated in contrast to the taste of that which is bitter or sour.

Until Adam sinned he was innocent and could have had but little, if any, true appreciation for his estate. Babies, in their innocence, know they are comfortable, but little appreciation for what created that comfort. Jesus said, "The one who loves most is the one who has been forgiven." The more we think about what God planned, the more sense this whole system makes.

Adam was not created to die. Death was his choice. He was not created to be sick but to live in health. He would have lived in health had he not disobeyed God. However, if Adam had not sinned he could not have had a proper appreciation for the garden in which he lived or for the One who put him there. We often hear it said: "I never really appreciated my health until I got sick."

CHAPTER TWO

Cause of Sickness

When Adam sinned, he brought death into the human family. In fact, Adam began to die the very day he partook of the fruit of the forbidden tree. Since that day, every one of Adam's descendants has been born under the sentence of death. Death, as a process, begins the day one is born. Living cells in our bodies are constantly dying and being replaced by new ones. When old cells die faster than they are being replaced by new ones, we begin to decline. In each person this happens at different times in various parts of the body. This is the natural process which ultimately leads to aging and then the death of the body. There are other factors involved, however, which make the pattern different in each individual. The pace of the process is determined by several factors.

Heredity

Some babies are born with healthy bodies; some are born sickly and infirm. Some of this has to do with the health of the mother and the circumstances of the birth, but much more is due to heredity. When healthy chromosomes and genes are passed on to children, healthy babies are born. Defective genes can also be passed on with the potential to develop various kinds of physical weakness. Geneticists working with animals have verified that good and bad traits can be passed from one generation to another. Long before this was called a science, Jacob was aware of this principle and developed a plan of breeding which would produce healthy cattle, with the markings he desired (Genesis 30). Utilizing this knowledge, Hitler tried to create a super race of people.

Adam and Eve were created perfect in every way. Their genes and chromosomes were not damaged or defective. They had the ability to produce a healthy race of human beings. But when they sinned, the principle of death and physical disease took hold, and created the potential to develop hereditary physical weaknesses. Every individual born in this world is the product of his own heredity, good or bad. Nothing can be done to escape the existence of these hereditary factors.

When a person meets Jesus, he comes with the body he has, weak or strong, sick or well. We come to Him as we are. Spiritually, we immediately become new, but physically we are the same. Death is still working in our body of flesh.

We are spiritually alive in a body subject to the law of death. God's ultimate plan for us includes a new body. "Our citizenship is in heaven from which we also eagerly wait for the Savior, the Lord Jesus Christ, who will transform our lowly body that it may be confirmed to His glorious body according to the working by which He is able even to subdue all things to Himself."

(Philippians 3:20-21) "This corruptible (body) must put on incorruption, and the mortal must put on immortality." (I Corinthians 15:53)

Environment

Health is affected not only by hereditary factors but also by environmental factors. There are many who are born into an environment which is hostile to good health. In many countries of this world I have watched man, women, and little children drink water from streams filled with refuse. Many are born, live, and die in the most unsanitary conditions imaginable.

Others may live in an environment which is physically sanitary, but filled with tension producing stress. This kind of an environment has a negative effect on the physical and emotional health of those who live in it. This is true for the Christian as well as the non-Christian. However, as we will see later, the Christian is much better equipped to cope with stressful situations.

Attitudes

A third factor which can influence physical health is attitude. Studies have indicated that as much as eighty-five percent of the physical problems people suffer are psychosomatic symptoms or physical illnesses brought on by attitudes such as hatred, jealousy, bitterness, unforgiveness, anger, fear and depression. Some believers have not learned to deal appropriately with these very real difficulties. As a result many suffer with debilitating physical problems brought on by wrong attitudes. Proverbs says: "jealousy is as rottenness of the bones." (14:30)... "A merry heart does good like a medicine." (17:22) The saying has it that laughter is the best medicine. In fact, recently studies have been published in support of this supposition. In my experience, attitude has a great deal to do with physical health.

Laws Which Govern Health

A fourth reason why Christians are sick may be ignorance of, or disregard for the laws which govern health. Diet, exercise, rest, posture, and fresh air all affect health. Eating too much or too little or the wrong things, not getting the right amount and kind of exercise, not getting adequate rest, not practicing good posture, and insufficient ventilation or polluted air all cause health problems.

If we are ignorant of those things which are bad for our health, or do not pay attention to working toward eliminating them from our lives, we will suffer the consequences. This is true for both believers and non-believers. Many blatantly disregard the laws of health and pray for healing only to find that "whatsoever person sows that shall he also reap." If we sow the seeds of physical corruption, we are sure to reap a harvest of physical difficulties.

Someone may say: "I know a person who never properly cared for his body and he lived to be 90 years old." Most of us have known such persons. However, this does not mean that the laws of health do not apply to some people. What is the explanation for the apparent exception? It is possible that this person had a very strong constitution and would have lived even longer if he had regarded the laws which govern good health. We also all know individuals born with a weak constitution, but who lived a long time by the mercy of God because they took proper care of their bodies and followed good health practices.

Demons

Finally, Scripture indicates that there are sicknesses which can be attributed to demons. Satan seems to have the power, under certain circumstances, to afflict people with disease. The gospel of Luke recounts the story of a woman identified as a daughter of Abraham of whom Jesus said, "Satan has bound for eighteen years." Luke says, "She had a spirit of infirmity," which prevented her from standing in an upright position. She may have suffered from a severe curvature of the spine. Jesus discerned that her condition was the result of a spirit which had "bound" her.

On another occasion Jesus identified an evil spirit as the cause of a deaf mute's problem. We cannot claim that every person who cannot talk or hear is held in the grip of a deaf or mute spirit. Nor can we say that all who suffer with curvature of the spine are possessed by a spirit of infirmity. However, we cannot rule out the possibility. The healing evangelist sometimes speaks to a spirit of infirmity while ministering to the sick, perhaps discerning hypochondria which is demonically induced. But, as we often see, when one evangelist is used in this manner, others try to copy what they have seen and heard and begin to label every sickness demonic. I have actually heard men attempt to cast out a spirit of appendicitis.

We cannot presume that all sickness is an indication of the presence of demon spirits. Some have taught this error and have brought hurt and confusion to the people of God. ✜ Having said that, it also should be said that we must always pray that the gift of discerning of spirits will be manifest when we minister to those who suffer from chronic physical conditions. Our Lord Jesus did "go about doing good and healing all who were oppressed of the devil." (Acts 10:38) It is possible for a Christian to "give place to the devil." (Ephesians 4:27). Harboring envy, bitterness, unforgiveness, hatred and evil thoughts toward anyone can open the door for a spirit of infirmity. Peter tells us to "resist the devil and he will flee" from us.

Perhaps this is the reason for James' word to the sick in the church: "Are any sick among you Christians? Let the sick call for the elders of the church, and let them anoint him with oil in the name of the Lord and the prayer of faith will save the sick and the Lord will raise him up." Note well: "Confess our sins to one another and pray one for another that you may be healed." There is an implication here that sin can open the door to sickness, perhaps to the activity of the devil.

In the context of healing, all sin must be confessed to those who minister healing. Why?

In order that if place has been given to Satan, that place can be reclaimed. I am personally acquainted with a number of cases in which physical problems have been completely healed once a sufferer dealt appropriately with personal sin. However, we cannot presume that all sickness is the result of sin in one's life. Sadly, there have been those who erroneously made such assumptions and have brought innocent people under a load of false guilt.

CHAPTER THREE

Free From the Fall

Christians are sick for the same reasons as non-Christians. Heredity, environment, attitude, and disregard for the laws governing health may result in illness and premature death for both believers and non-believers. What, then, about the redemption of the body? Did not Jesus die on the cross to cancel the debt of sin and redeem mankind from sin's consequences? The answer is **yes!**, not a simple yes, but a yes requiring some qualification.

I am fully convinced that God's ultimate plan for all of His people is complete deliverance from the effects of the fall, (including the physical consequences known as sickness). However, a careful study of the Scriptures reveals the difference between God's immediate plan and His ultimate plan.

For example, God's ultimate plan for Abraham's seed (Genesis 15), was that in it all of the nations of the earth would be blessed. Paul points out that the word "seed" is singular, and that we are to understand that God was speaking about Jesus who was the "Seed" of Abraham. In Christ Jesus all of the nations of the earth are to be blessed. This was not God's immediate plan. However, it was and is His *ultimate* plan.

The question is: when Isaiah said, referring to Jesus, "with His stripes we are healed" was he stating God's immediate or His ultimate plan for the nation of Israel? This prophecy was seven hundred years before the coming of the Messiah. So, we know it was not God's immediate plan for Abraham's progeny. It was His ultimate plan. John says of Jesus, "He came to His own..." referring to His coming to the nation of Israel. They rejected Him, beat Him, and ultimately crucified Him. Did their actions nullify God's ultimate intention? No! Their actions set up conditions under which God could begin the fulfillment of the rest of the promise He made to Abraham. "All of the nations of the earth shall be blessed." The rejection of Christ by the Jews opened the door for us Gentiles, and our acceptance of Messiah will ultimately open the door again for them (Romans 11).

The way God works is to state His ultimate intention for people and then very deliberately begin to execute it. If there is not full belief or acceptance of God's plan, it may be delayed, but nothing nullifies it. John says: "As many as received Him to them gave He the right to become the children of God, to those who believe in His name." (John 1:12) Because Israel rejected the Messiah the nation was rejected by God from entering into the blessing promised to Abraham's descendants, but only for a season. Those who, at the time, did receive Christ entered into the blessings promised to the children of Abraham.

What does all of this mean? God's ultimate intention for His redeemed children is that they experience healing – complete healing – physical, spiritual, emotional, moral, and material. The paradise lost through the sin of the first Adam is to be completely restored. The whole race was in him: therefore, all were affected by his sin. Total healing will be the ultimate experience of all of those who are in the second Adam, the Lord Jesus Christ.

Meanwhile, we live in a world system which is under the curse which God pronounced on Adam because of his sin. Sin, sickness, pain and death rule. Believer and nonbeliever alike suffer because of that curse which has not yet been removed.

What, then, is different in the experience of the believer and the nonbeliever? When a believer suffers, he suffers in hope? In the hope of experiencing the mercy gift of divine healing. This gift is not automatic or universal, but it may occur and often does as we pray. Why does it not happen every time? Perhaps Paul has answered this question best. He said: "We are waiting for the redemption of the body." (Romans 8:23) Full redemption has not yet occurred. Occasionally, we receive a foretaste, a sort of interest on our ultimate in-heritance: we are supernaturally healed.

Ultimately, all who are in Christ will have a new body and a new life. While experience shows us that this is not God's immediate plan, there is no question but that it is His ultimate plan. Every child of God will have a new body, and all who are in Christ will enter into the blessing of eternal life and health. John says: "no more sadness, sorrow, pain or death." (Revelation 21) Meanwhile, we travel through a veil of tears, some of us more than others. It has been my observation over the years that what my earthly father told me was true when he said: "Son, people do not suffer because they are bad, nor are they blessed because they are good." Good people suffer, and at times, bad people seem to prosper.

The Psalmist observed this seeming inequity and said: "My feet had almost stumbled; my steps had nearly slipped, for I was envious of the boastful when I saw the prosperity of the wicked." (Psalm 73:1-3) Later he said that when he came into the sanctuary of God, he understood their end. The day of reckoning is coming. The books will be balanced. In this life there is not equity. Good people may suffer, bad ones may prosper. But, what of the end? Is there a day of judgment? Will we all stand before God and give an account of the deeds done in this body of flesh? Yes, we will.

I cannot tell you that you will be healed every time you get sick. I cannot tell you that your earthly life will be lengthened. I cannot promise that you will be wealthy. But I can promise that if you will observe the laws of health and wealth, you can be as healthy and prosperous as you have the potential to be. If you will serve the Lord, you can expect His special favor on your life here on this earth and ultimately a home in heaven.

CHAPTER FOUR

Two Specific Reasons Why So Few Christians are Healed

When Jesus ministered to the sick, the demon possessed, and the oppressed they were healed. What was different about His ministry? Let us take a careful look at His ministry and listen to what He said "The words I speak are not my words, they are the words of Him that sent me... I did not come to do my will but the will of Him that sent me...The Son of man can do nothing of His own volition. He can do only what He sees His Father do." How interesting. Jesus did nothing of His own volition. There were times when He healed everyone present. At other times He healed only one among many. He did only what His Father told Him to do.

After His resurrection He called His disciples together and said to them, "As my Father has sent me into the world, even so send I you." He sent me to do His will – I send you to do my will. I did not act of my own volition, I did what my Father told me to do. I want you to do the same. After this He breathed on them and said, "Receive the Holy Ghost." When we do what Jesus did in obeying His Father, we can expect the same results He had in seeing the sick healed.

While on the earth Jesus lived as a mortal filled with the Holy Spirit. He was not a superman. He could only do what His Father told Him to do. He had the power to still storms, calm angry waves, heal the sick, raise the dead and cast out devils. However, a careful study will reveal that the power He possessed was only manifested when He had been given specific authority to exercise it.

To His disciples He said, "Wait in Jerusalem for the power of the Holy Spirit...do not leave there until this happens." I am going to my Father and He will give me the Holy Spirit to give to you. You will have power to do the same things I have done. Remember, I listened to my Father and He told me when to use this power. Listen to me and I will tell you when you are to exercise the power that will come upon you.

Did His disciples get the message? I believe they did. They waited in Jerusalem for the empowering of the Holy spirit. This happened a few days after our Lord's ascension. They began to do exactly what the Lord told them. In acts three we are told that Peter and John were going to the temple to pray at the hour of prayer. This they did as this same time every day. Lying near the Beautiful Gate of the temple was a forty year old paralytic who was brought there daily. Peter had passed him before – Jesus Himself had gone through that gate. On this day Peter said: "Silver and gold have I none but such as I have give I thee, in the authority of Jesus Christ of Nazareth rise up and walk." His feet and ankle bones received strength immediately – he was completely healed.

What did Peter have this day that he had not had the day before? **Authority!** Specific authority to bring healing to the paralytic man.

This was not an isolated case. The same thing occurred in the ministry of the Apostle Paul in Acts 16:16.

What is the point? If we are to see people healed in answer to our prayers we must minister as Jesus ministered, that is, we must know that He has authorized us to do what we attempt to do. Much doubt, unbelief, and outright skepticism have been generated by well meaning people who attempt to do what they have not been authorized to do. Someone wisely has said, "The presence of a need does not indicate that one is commissioned to act." Remember the words of our Lord, "I can do nothing of my own volition." John 5:30 Neither can we. Is there a need? Yes. Am I authorized to meet it? I am always authorized to pray about the need – I may be commissioned to meet it.

CHAPTER FIVE

Greater Works

Jesus said: "He that believeth on me the works that I do shall he do and greater works than these shall he do." (John 14:12,13) What kind of works did Jesus do? He healed the sick, raised the dead, opened the eyes of the blind and did many other spectacular things. Then He said that anyone who believed in Him would do the works He had done and even greater things.

Have you opened any blind eyes lately Have you raised anyone from the dead? How about hearing? Have opened deaf ears? Jesus said that believers will do all of these things. Are you a believer? Yes! If you are trusting Jesus as your savior you are a believer. But, in spite of the fact that we even believe that God heals, only rarely do we see it ~~happy~~ happen.

What is the problem? Is there an answer? I believe there is. The answer will be found in careful study of the little phrase "greater works than these shall you do." Can anyone do greater works than Jesus did? He said we could and would.

What are these" greater works'? I believe the greater works of which Jesus spoke are opening spiritually blind eyes – raising the spiritually dead to spiritual life. The greater works are spiritual works. Raise a man from physical death to physical life and he will die again. Raise a man from spiritual death to spiritual life and he never dies. This is the greater miracle.

When Jesus was on the earth, He healed the sick and delivered the oppressed as a demonstration of the presence and power of the Kingdom of God. When He sent out His disciples, He gave them the authority to make disciples of the nations, offering eternal life to all who would accept. There is a vast difference between the spectacular and the miraculous. The salvation of the lost may not be spectacular but it is certainly miraculous.

I have carefully observed the charismatic renewal since its beginning. Though I was raised a classical Pentecostal, I have been part of the charismatic renewal from its start. The renewal was a wonderful move of God. Many came into a loving relationship with the living Lord Jesus. They came alive in God. I thank God for the charismatic movement. However, it was not characterized by evangelistic or missionary zeal.

I was brought up under the influence of such teachers as Donald Gee, the great Pentecostal preacher from Great Britain, and Raymond TJ. Richey of Houston, Texas. Richey would come to the city of Eureka Springs, Arkansas to the great old Tri-State Camp Meetings. People came from miles around to hear the gospel, and the Lord confirmed His word with signs following. I remember seeing crutches, canes, and braces laid out from one side of the platform to the other. People were being healed and many were being saved. In those days healing was seen as a means to an end. Healing followed the ministries of missionaries and evangelists By miraculous signs God validated the ministry of those who spoke and ministered on His behalf.

Later on, healing became an end in itself. Individuals began to specialize in the ministry of healing, a specialization not found in the Bible. People began to seek signs. What did Jesus say regarding sign seekers? He said, I will give you a sign, but it will not be the one you are seeking. As the church began to specialize in the ministry of healing, with little regard for the salvation of the lost, we saw a diminishing of verifiable healings and miracles. They did not stop completely, but diminished to a trickle. As healing waned, many began to preach more and more about faith and miracles and how to "get yours" The more we preached the less we saw.

For six years I served as pastor of prayer and counseling at the Church on the Rock in Rockwall, Texas, where Larry Lea was the pastor.

During its first five years, that church experienced unusual growth. Pastor Larry rarely said anything about healing. Yet, we saw many bona fide healings. Blind eyes, deaf ears, cancer – many kinds of sicknesses were healed. People were not called to the front for prayer for healing. Healing was happening in the congregation as the simple gospel was preached.

The main emphasis was on "greater things," i.e., the salvation of the lost. As long as we emphasized the greater things, we saw the lesser things. Once we began to focus on the lesser l things and began to treat them as though they were the greater things, we actually saw less of both.

I am convinced that if the church is to see a return of the miraculous we must focus our attention upon the salvation of the lost. We must major in majors and minor in minors. WE must have an adjustment in our sense of values. WE must call greater what God calls greater and what HE calls lesser we must call lesser.

Will there be a return of the supernatural?
Yes, I believe there will be. When will it be?
When we turn our attention once again to the
mission of the church, "Go into all the world
and share the good news with every person."

CHAPTER SIX

Believers' Advantages

Believers are sick and infirm for the same reasons as are unbelievers. Some are born with strong bodies, others with weak bodies. Heredity works the same in all. Environment, working conditions, stressful situations, and lifestyle are all determining factors in health. A bad attitude can have extremely negative effects on physical health. This, of course, will be the same in believers as nonbelievers.

In view of this, what advantage has the believer over the unbeliever? Much, in every way. Believers have the blessing of knowing God as their Father. Their mental and emotional condition should be better than that of the unbeliever, thus contributing, in general, to better health. The wise believer will abstain from a lifestyle which may contribute to poor health. Through the grace of God, he will be delivered from smoking, drinking, and illicit sexual conduct, all of which produce negative consequences on one's well-being: physical, mental, emotional, spiritual, and material. The believer knows of God's ability to heal in response to the prayer of faith. Even when suffering, the believer has not only the hope of being healed, he has the hope of heaven if he should die.

What of the person who has lived an immoral life as a non believer and is already suffering the effects of that lifestyle in his or her physical body? Is there any hope for such a person? Yes, there is hope! Our God is a good God and often, in His mercy, nullifies the effects of a sinful life. This is not guaranteed by the promises of God, but it does happen. What can be done? Correct everything that can be corrected, and pray for God's mercy. He is a God whose mercy endures forever. Come before Him boldly. Many have been restored. You may be also.

A word to the faithful believer who has a chronic or terminal illness: In my lifetime I have witnessed many supernatural healings. One afternoon several years ago, I was routinely visiting a member of my church who was ill in the hospital. I was introduced to the person occupying the other bed in the room. I was told she was a minister of the gospel who just recently had been operated on for cancer. She had been steadily growing worse. I was asked to pray for her and did. While I was praying, the Lord spoke to me and said: "Tell her she has many more days to serve me." I gave her that word and bade her good day. The next time I visited the hospital she was not there. I did not know what had happened to her.

About two years later I was in a neighboring town. As I walked across a parking lot an elderly lady came toward me inquiring: "Do you remember me?" My response was: "I'm sorry, I do not believe I do." She introduced herself and told me she was the person for whom I had prayed two years before. She told me she had been healed immediately and had suffered no more cancer. Many give similar testimonies. And all of us who are honest have to tell of times when we prayed and nothing happened. I remember hearing the late Kathryn Kuhlman say: "When I get to heaven, there is one question I want to ask my Father. I want to ask Him why some of the people for whom I prayed were healed and some were not"

I cannot explain why the righteous suffer, why some are healed and some are not. God has not chosen to reveal this to us. However, one day as I was praying I received a word which I believe was from the Lord. "Son, you have wondered why some of your prayers are answered and others are not. The law of relativity operates in the spiritual realm the same as in the physical realm." He knew I did not know much about the law of relativity. But knowing what I understood, He chose to teach me through my limited comprehension.

The law of relativity states in essence that all things are related. Nothing happens in a vacuum or isolated from anything else that happens. If there is an action at any point there is a corresponding reaction everywhere. It is like throwing a rock in a pond. God was saying to me: "When I do something at one point it affects things in many other places. I do not always do what you want me to do because of how it will affect other things along the chain."

His words to me gave me a new understanding of what Paul had said: "All things work together..." Things are not working separately, they are working together, and because of the way one thing affects another, God does not always do what seems right to us. This may not help you, but it helped me. When I pray about a matter earnestly in faith, I know that what happens will be the will of God, especially when I pray, "Thy will be done."

CHAPTER SEVEN

A Word to the Unconverted

Trust in the Lord, repent and turn to Him with all your heart and life. Make Jesus Lord of your life and pray for a miracle. Will God answer? Yes, He will save you the moment you put your trust in Jesus.

Someone may ask; "How do I do this?" Just pray this prayer from the bottom of your heart:

Lord Jesus, I have sinned against heaven and before You. I am sorry. Please forgive me and cleanse me from all of my sins. From this moment I will claim You as my Savior, because I believe You died to save me from all of my sins. From this day on I will do Your will as You give me the strength. Amen!

Read your Bible and talk to God every day. As you do, you will grow in your knowledge of Him. The Better you know Him, the more you will love Him, and the more you love Him, the more faithfully you will obey Him. Where God is concerned, "obedience is better than sacrifice." God is pleased to bless with special favor those who "delight greatly in His commandments." (Psalm 112:1-2)

National Call to Prayer

If you would like to receive daily prayer alerts from National Call to Prayer, please use this link: http://www.nationalcalltoprayer.org

One Final Thought...

If you have purchased this book on Amazon and it makes a difference in your life ... please consider writing a review to encourage others in their search for answers.

Recommended Reading

Law of Prayer –B. J. Willhite

Why Pray? - B. J. Willhite

How Much Faith Does it Take to Move the Hand of God? - B. J. Willhite

Could You Not Tarry One Hour? -

Dr. Larry Lea

How to Pray for Your Loved Ones – (Also available in Spanish & French)

Dr. Kathy Casto

There is a Word for Every Storm –

Dr. Kathy Casto

The Basics of Hospice Chaplain Ministry – Chaplain John Casto

Notes

Notes

_____

_____

_____

_____

_____

_____

_____

_____

_____

_____

_____

_____

_____

_____

_____

_____

_____

Made in United States
Orlando, FL
01 December 2024

54752629R00033